Learning Disorders and Disabilities

A GUIDE FOR PARENTS

By

Martin Baren, MD
University of California, Irvine

MEDICAL CONSULTANT

Martin T. Stein, MD
Professor of Pediatrics
University of California, San Diego

EDUCATIONAL CONSULTANT

Dennis Kreil, PhD
Director of Pupil Services
Placentia-Yorba Linda Unified School District

© Copyright 2000 by Health InfoNet Inc.
231 Market Place, #331, San Ramon, CA 94583
Phone: 800-HIN-1947
Consumer's Website: HINhealthbooks.com
Professional's Website: HINbooks.com

ISBN 1-885274-59-9
MADE IN THE U.S.A.

About the Author

Dr. Martin Baren is Clinical Professor of Pediatrics at the University of California, Irvine, College of Medicine. He has written numerous publications and articles on behavioral problems and learning disorders in children. Dr. Baren has been in private practice specializing in Developmental, Behavioral, and Educational Pediatrics for 28 years. He has also been a medical consultant for learning disabilities to several school districts.

Editorial Consultant: Robin Solit

Design: Randy Heyman

Illustrations: David Lobenberg, Peg Magovern, Todd Leonardo, Lori Tyminski, Andree Policicchio

TABLE OF CONTENTS

What Are Learning Disorders? 4

What Causes Learning Disorders? 6

Other Learning Problems 8

Academic Problem Areas 10

When Do Learning Disorders Start? 14

Diagnosing Learning Disorders 15

How to Help Your Child Succeed 18

Laws Covering Learning Disorders 22

Does Medication Help? 24

Good Grades and Self-Esteem 26

Your Child's Future 27

Summary 28

Glossary of Terms 29

Additional Information 30

Books and Articles 31

WHAT ARE LEARNING DISORDERS?

Learning disorders are school-related problems that keep children from learning as well as they should. Learning disorders often continue into the adult years.

These difficulties are thought to be due to problems the brain has with handling information (processing skills). Some children with learning disorders have trouble listening or speaking. Others have problems with reading, writing, math, or spelling. Many students may struggle with several of these problems.

Learning disorders is a term used to describe any problem originating in the brain that may affect a child's ability to learn or perform at school.

Learning Disorder or Learning Disability

These terms often overlap when used by teachers, other education professionals, and doctors. Some of the labels used to classify learning disorders may be confusing.

The ultimate goal is to find out why your child is having trouble at school, and not to concentrate on the labels.

Learning Disorder: Any learning difficulty caused by **central nervous system** (brain) problems.

Learning Disability (LD): A specific type of learning disorder that results in a significant difference between a child's natural ability (IQ) and his or her level of achievement, as defined by federal and state laws. This difference is a matter of degree as determined by **psychoeducational testing** performed by psychologists and educators.

Current federal law defines learning-disabled children as having a disorder in *"one or more of the basic psychological processes involving understanding or using spoken or written language which manifests itself in an imperfect ability to listen, think, speak, read, write, or do mathematical calculations."*

This learning disability definition includes children with brain injury and dysfunction, as well as dyslexia. However, it excludes visual, hearing and motor handicaps, mental retardation, emotional disturbances, and environmental, cultural, or economic disadvantages.

Learning disabilities entitle children to federal, state, and local school special education assistance.

WHAT CAUSES LEARNING DISORDERS?

Most definitions assume that learning disorders are due to some type of central nervous system (brain) dysfunction, damage, or structural abnormality.

- Some learning disorders are genetic (inherited). These problems can run in families. For example, families might have several members who have trouble with reading or math.

- Exposure to toxins during pregnancy, such as the use of drugs or alcohol by the mother, can also cause learning disorders in a child.

- Most often the causes of the learning disorders are unknown.

Since the central nervous system contains billions of nerve cells and complicated connections, it is a wonder that we do not see more children with specific problems in the area of learning.

Some Brain Functions That May Go Wrong

Language processing. The child has difficulty reading, sounding out words, or recognizing the meaning of words. The child also may have problems with expressing thoughts and understanding things he or she hears.

Memory. The child has difficulty remembering letters, word meanings, spelling, and math facts. Memory problems also cause difficulty with following directions and understanding the meaning of a paragraph or story.

Visual-spatial. The child has trouble with matching designs, geometric shapes, and shapes of letters. This especially may be seen with writing and producing work.

Motor coordination. The child has difficulty with finger and hand control. This may cause problems with handwriting.

Sequencing and time awareness. The child has problems with remembering things in order or difficulties with time management and things such as dates, seasons, etc.

Attention-Deficit/Hyperactivity Disorder

Attention-Deficit/Hyperactivity Disorder (ADHD) is not a learning disorder, but often accompanies learning problems. About half of the children who have learning disabilities also have ADHD. Up to one third of children with ADHD also have learning disabilities.

Children with ADHD are more likely to have trouble with academic performance rather than with specific reading or math skills. They usually have problems producing and finishing their work, following directions, listening, and with organizational and study skills.

Learning disabilities may be due to problems with the structure of the brain. ADHD involves the chemical-electrical energy necessary to make things work.

Good News: Some children who show learning disorders at a very early age may only be a bit delayed in the growth of their central nervous system. These children may do much better as they get older.

OTHER LEARNING PROBLEMS

Not all learning problems are caused by learning disorders. Some children have extrinsic (external) problems that can get in the way of doing well at school.

Extrinsic (External) Problems

- Neglect or serious family troubles.

- Cultural differences (when a child comes from a family that is different from others in the school).

- Physical problems (on-going illness, eyesight, or hearing problems).

- Nutritional background (poor nourishment as an infant or lack of a daily breakfast).

- School placement (differences in teaching or learning styles between the child and the teacher or school).

It is important to be certain that there are no extrinsic (external) problems causing a child's difficulties in school. This should be done before searching for intrinsic (internal) problems, which the child is born with.

A child with an intrinsic learning disorder may also be influenced by extrinsic factors. It is important to identify all contributing factors.

Whether a child's learning problems are intrinsic, extrinsic, or both, the parents, schools, and the family doctors must do everything they can to support and help the child.

How Common Are Learning Disorders?

About 3 to 5 percent of children have specific learning disabilities that fit into federal, state, and local guidelines. However, as many as 25 percent of children do poorly in school because of all types of learning disorders.

Large numbers of children are never diagnosed or treated. This is because they do not show the specified difference between ability and academic achievement designated by law as a "Specific Learning Disability." Many of these children suffer in school, both academically and socially.

Public schools are setting up more early intervention programs to identify and work with children who are having difficulty acquiring needed literacy skills.

Your Child is Unique: No one child is like another when it comes to learning disorders. This is why it is important to correctly identify and treat each child individually.

ACADEMIC PROBLEM AREAS

Schooling is a very important activity of childhood. Success or failure in school makes a big difference in whether children feel good or bad, and also in their feelings about themselves (self-esteem).

- 75 percent of untreated children with learning disorders may not go to college. Many of these students may develop social and behavioral problems.

- A large number of these children also may do poorly in the labor market, if not diagnosed and treated.

- Children who fail at school due to learning problems often feel anxious, depressed, or worthless. They are at great risk for carrying these feelings into adulthood.

- Children with learning disorders can develop social problems unless they get help early.

Specific Academic Problem Areas

Children who have learning disorders can have problems in the following areas, or in a combination of them:

- Reading
- Writing
- Math
- Spelling

Reading Problems

Young readers must be aware and recognize the sounds of our language. They must also recognize (decode) letters, syllables, and words. This is probably the most important skill that is necessary in terms of reading. Learning the meanings of words and paragraphs (comprehension) is also important.

Reading disorders are usually caused by problems with language, memory, and attention. Occasionally, they are caused by visual processing problems.

Children with reading difficulties often have problems with such skills as rhyming and naming items quickly. However, good readers also have to develop their skills in vocabulary and grammar.

What is Dyslexia?

Dyslexia is a specific language problem involving reading, as well as writing and spelling.

It does not cause the reversing of letters, words, or numbers. Dyslexia does not mean that children write backwards. Many children make these errors as beginners, then grow out of them.

Dyslexia is characterized by a lack of ability to recognize differences in sounds, put sounds together into words, and recognize which letters or symbols are connected with what sounds.

Current thinking about dyslexia is changing. It may just be a form of reading disability, and not a specific disorder unto itself.

Writing Problems (Dysgraphia)

Learning to write is a complicated task involving 10 to 15 developmental skills. If several of these skills are lacking, poor handwriting may result. Some of these problem areas include:

- Fine motor coordination difficulties.

- Lack of organization and planning.

- Memory and language problems.

- Trouble paying attention.

- Visual-spatial difficulties.

Math Problems

Learning disorders in math are harder to overcome than reading problems. Children with math problems may have trouble understanding what it means to add, subtract, multiply, or divide. They may forget basic math facts, and find word problems difficult. Shapes and geometry may be extremely difficult for them. Math is a very complex field, and learning problems may come in various areas.

Spelling Problems

Spelling problems are common among children with learning disorders. They usually go hand-in-hand with reading, handwriting, and attention problems.

Some children with learning disorders may be excellent spellers when they need to remember 10 to 20 words for a test. However, they often will not be able to use these words in a sentence two weeks later. This is especially true for children with ADHD.

The Bad News: Many people with learning disorders never become good spellers.

The Good News: Using a computer spelling program or spelling machine can help manage this problem.

WHEN DO LEARNING DISORDERS START?

Some children with diagnosed learning disorders may have had poor language development at an early age. Many children will be identified by a preschool teacher as having a risk for learning disorders.

Some children show problems with learning letters, numbers, and sounds beginning in kindergarten. A child who has difficulties with rhyming often can be predicted to develop reading difficulties later on.

Other children may do well in school until fourth or fifth grade. Until then, they were asked to decode (take in) information. Starting around the fourth grade, children must also encode (produce work) such as in class and homework writing assignments.

Some learning disorders may not show themselves until the student is exposed to more advanced language work (including foreign languages), abstract math, and science in middle school, high school, and college.

Learning disorders are not always present at a certain age or grade. However, children who still have reading disorders by the fourth grade often continue to experience these problems in middle and high school.

DIAGNOSING LEARNING DISORDERS

It is important to know if your child has a learning disorder, and if so, which kind. You may meet with various professionals during the diagnosing process.

People Who Diagnose Learning Disorders

- **Teachers.** Often a teacher is the first person to notice that a child is having trouble in school. Very often, preschool teachers are the first ones to supply this information.

- **School Specialists.** Your child's school usually has a psychologist or learning specialists.

- **Doctors.** Your doctor can help by evaluating your child's physical health. You may also be referred to a doctor who is specially trained in treating learning disorders.

- **Private Learning Specialists and Educational Psychologists.** You and your child may be working with specialists outside the school system. These specialists can help define your child's problem by special tests and observations.

Myth: *"More boys than girls have learning disorders."*

Fact: Boys' behavior may alert teachers to a learning problem, but just as many girls as boys show these disorders.

Health Assessment

Determining a child's learning disorder requires some detective work. Your child's doctor can help by conducting a physical exam and taking a family history.

Your child's doctor may want to know:

- What health and safety conditions may have affected your developing child while you were pregnant?

- What was your child like as an infant, in terms of feeding, colic, sleeping, or trouble in preschool?

- Has your child had any delays in the development of language skills? (This is very important.)

- How does your child get along with teachers, adults, and other children? How is your child doing in school?

- Do other family members have learning disorders?

- What is your child's overall health - illnesses, exposure to poisons, allergies or asthma, eating habits, vision, and hearing problems? Repeated ear infections may interfere with a child's normal language development.

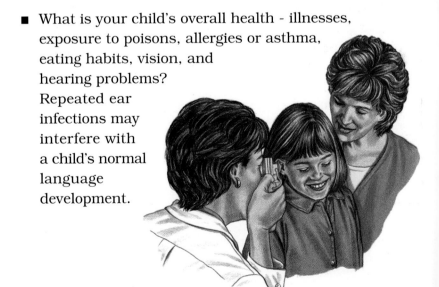

Having Your Child Evaluated

Testing is needed to identify your child's learning problem. The tests may be given either at your child's school or through a private educational testing agency.

Tests such as magnetic resonance imaging (MRI) or computed tomography (CT) scanning of the brain do not help diagnose learning disorders. These tests may show an abnormal condition in some people, but they are not used to diagnose learning disorders at the present time.

Common Tests

- Tests for specific academic skills (reading, writing, and math).

- Tests of the central nervous system to find out how the child receives and processes information **(psychoeducational and neurodevelopmental testing)**. These tests may include evaluations for intelligence, memory, language, sequencing, attention, motor skills, and visual-spatial skills.

- Social and emotional tests.

- Physical tests, such as ear and eye exams.

HOW TO HELP YOUR CHILD SUCCEED

Once a child has been diagnosed with a learning disorder, it is best to tell him or her exactly what is going on. At first, the child may feel badly. However, it is often a relief for the parent and child to be able to give a name to the problems that have been occurring at school.

The school, teachers, family, and child can all work together to help understand and manage the disability. Giving a name to the problem should not be an excuse for not working hard or for reoccurring behavior problems.

What the Teachers and School Can Do

Teachers with special training can help the child develop skills that are lacking. The school can give a child special education instruction or modify the classroom curriculum and testing to meet the child's needs.

Things that the teacher can do to help a child succeed in spite of learning disorders include:

- Allow the child to progress at his or her own speed.

- Do not accuse the child of laziness, sloppiness, or not paying attention.

- Avoid giving long verbal instructions. Give the child written instructions.

- Allow the child to sit at the front of the classroom.

- Do not force the child to read in front of the class until he or she is ready to do so.

- Have the child underline while reading.

- Supply a copy of class notes for a child who has difficulties with writing, memory, or attention skills.

- If a child has problems with language or memory, make sure he or she receives visual information.

- Use graph paper for the child who has difficulty writing down math problems.

- Allow a child who has problems with writing to dictate the work before having to produce it in writing. Allow parents to help by typing the child's dictated work.

- Give a list of the homework assignments to the child if he or she has problems copying.

- Ask for the homework if the child forgets to turn it in.

- Limit the amount of homework assignments so that the child does not have hours of work to do.

- Divide long-term assignments into smaller parts.

- Do not mark down a child's work for spelling errors or sloppiness, if learning disorders are causing the problem.

- Divide tests into smaller parts, with a limited number of questions per section.

- Allow extra time for the child to take a test, and in some cases give a test in a separate room without distractions.

- Make sure the child understands the test questions. The test should be on specific subject knowledge and not on the child's ability to take the test.

- Do not require perfection on certain tasks (handwriting, spelling) before giving the child more complex material. Do not allow the problem in one area to interfere with the child's ability to go on to higher learning.

Additional things the school can do to help include:

- A child with difficulties in visual memory or reading will do better listening to materials. Books on tape can greatly help with reading. Most textbooks and commonly used novels are available on cassette tapes.

- Allow the child to use calculators, electronic spelling machines, and tape recorders in school.

What You as a Parent Can Do

Your attitude and active help can make a big difference in your child's success in school.

- Be positive. Boost your child's confidence by emphasizing his or her strengths.

- Be sure your child knows that the learning disorder is not anyone's fault.

- Celebrate your child's successes, one at a time. Each small step is a victory.

- Be active in identifying and treating your child's learning disorder. You are your child's best supporter.

- Find out what professional help and services are available at your child's school.

- Learn about the problems mentioned in this booklet, the educational laws, and the treatments available.

Develop an **I.E.P.** (Individualized Education Program) with your child's teacher and other school professionals as needed. The I.E.P. is designed to meet the specific needs of your child. It includes the goals to meet your child's educational, social, emotional, and behavioral needs in school - and how these goals may be attained.

As a parent, there are a number of techniques that will help your child a great deal.

- Work with your child's teacher. If the teacher is not taking an active approach, discuss the problem and develop new ideas with the teacher.

- Monitor your child's relationship with the teacher, and be aware of other available teachers who may also be able work with your child.

- Read aloud to your child.

- Provide your child with a special study space in a quiet location with good lighting.

- Supply your child with a homework assignment notebook, to be checked daily by the teacher and parent.

- Encourage your child to learn computer skills early, especially if he or she has writing problems.

- Give your child a tape recorder. Have him or her "talk" a report into the tape recorder first, and then have it typed or written. This can be fun, and it is highly effective in encouraging your child's thoughts to flow.

What Your Child Can Do

A child often feels very frustrated because of learning problems. However, your child can play an important part in finding ways to manage these problems.

- Your child can learn to tell others what he or she needs to learn properly.

- Your child can form study groups with friends.

- Your child can learn to ask questions so that every school assignment is clear.

LAWS COVERING LEARNING DISORDERS

Several specific laws cover your child's rights when it comes to getting help for learning disorders:

- **PL94-142** (Education for All Handicapped Children Act of 1975).

- **PL101-476** (Individuals with Disabilities Educational Act of 1990 - IDEA).

- **PL105-17** (update of IDEA in 1997).

Individuals with Disabilities Educational Act (IDEA) is the federal law that is currently in use. It states that *"a child with a disability is a child with mental retardation, hearing impairments (including deafness), speech or language impairments, visual impairments (including blindness), serious emotional disturbance, orthopedic impairments, autism, traumatic brain injury, other health impairments, or **specific learning disabilities**; and who, by reason thereof, needs special education and related services."*

IDEA outlines the public schools' responsibilities for providing a free and appropriate education to all children, including those with disabilities. Specific learning disabilities are one type of disability covered under the IDEA.

Laws and the basic definitions of learning disorders and disabilities are changing. So are the ways in which learning disordered children are being helped.

Fewer children are isolated in special education classes. More schools now follow **full inclusion**, where the child learns right along with other children. This movement is still being studied for how well it meets its goals.

In the future, all children with learning problems may be provided with needed assistance regardless of whether they meet specific guidelines.

Do the Laws Apply to a Gifted Child?

The law also requires that schools help a child who is very smart, yet still has a learning disorder.

Let's say, for example, a seventh grade child has an IQ of 140 (very high), yet is reading at only a seventh grade level. The high IQ indicates that the child should be reading at a high school or college level. Officially this discrepancy between ability (IQ score) and achievement (reading level) entitles the child to federally mandated special education help.

However, some school systems may not help the gifted child, reasoning that he or she is doing "well enough" no matter what test scores show. The current system for helping learning-disordered children does not always meet the needs of all children. Parents need to play an active role in getting the proper help.

How Is a Child Eligible for Help?

- Under IDEA, a child may be eligible for help if there is a large difference between ability and academic achievement (reading, math, etc.). A child may also be eligible under IDEA-B if he or she has a chronic health problem (including ADHD) that limits the educational performance (listening, following directions, organizing work, completing assignments).

- A child may also have an academic program or curriculum modified to meet his or her needs under the Civil Rights Laws (Section 504 of the Rehabilitation Act of 1973 and Americans With Disabilities Act of 1990 - ADA). This is especially necessary with children who have ADHD.

DOES MEDICATION HELP?

Some doctors give medications for certain problems associated with learning disorders. Children with ADHD, for example, are often given medications such as *Adderall, DextroStat* or *Dexedrine* (dextroamphetamine), or *Ritalin* (methylphenidate).

These medications do not make a child read or do math better. However, they may help a child perform better. They also may improve a child's memory skills, and help him or her finish more work in a timely manner.

If a child is depressed because of the trouble resulting from learning problems, antidepressant medication may help.

The decision to medicate a child is an important one. No child should take strong medications unnecessarily. Yet these medications may help some children. Make this decision with your child's doctor and learning specialists.

Therapies <u>Not</u> Proven to Work

- Anti-motion sickness medication *(Dramamine)*, sometimes given for dyslexia.

- Tinted lenses on eye glasses.

- Dietary supplements (vitamins, minerals).

- *Neurofeedback* and *biofeedback* therapy.

- "Vestibular dysfunction" treatment for inner ear.

- Eye muscle exercises.

- Occupational therapy (except may be helpful in some children with writing difficulties due to motor problems).

GOOD GRADES AND SELF-ESTEEM

As we try to help the children cope with their learning disorders and do well in school, we must also work with their feelings about themselves.

Children with learning problems are sometimes criticized by teachers, other children, their brothers and sisters, and even by their own parents. These negative remarks can destroy children's good feelings about themselves.

Ways to Increase Your Child's Self-Esteem

- Focus on your child's strengths. If your child is good at art, drama, music, or mechanical activities, provide many chances for your child to participate in these activities.

- Enroll an older learning-disordered child in vocational training courses offered by school districts (such as barber or beauty school, computer repair, or auto repair), if your child shows interest in them.

- Allow your child to see a psychological counselor on a regular basis.

- Continue to provide positive encouragement for your child, and avoid criticizing.

YOUR CHILD'S FUTURE

Knowledge of learning disorders is rapidly changing. Definitions are changing. Diagnostic tests, educational legislation, and therapies are also changing.

Because of these continuing changes, some children may not get the help they need.

This is why it is important for you as a parent to work with your child's school administrators and teachers to take active steps to help your child, even if he or she does not fit into specific guidelines.

Many children with learning problems will become adults who have problems with reading, writing, math, or spelling. If they are helped during their early school years, children can develop skills to cope with their learning weaknesses. This will help them lead positive and successful lives.

SUMMARY

- Finding out that your child has a learning disorder can be discouraging at first. Yet, knowing the reason for your child's problems at school can be a relief.

- As your child's most powerful supporter, you as a parent can make a big difference in your child's self-esteem and success in school.

- Make sure your child gets properly diagnosed by the appropriate medical and learning professionals.

- Have your doctor take a family history and give your child a complete physical exam, as well as proper neuro-developmental tests, when necessary.

- If your child has been diagnosed with a learning disability, take advantage of federal and local funding and special programs.

- Know the specific laws that cover your child's rights when it comes to getting help for learning disorders.

- Work with your child's school counselors, teachers, and learning specialists to create an effective program that will help your child.

- Provide positive encouragement for your child.

GLOSSARY OF TERMS

Attention Deficit Hyperactivity Disorder (ADHD)
A condition characterized by hyperactive and impulsive behavior or by problems with attention span.

Central Nervous System
The brain and spinal cord.

Dysgraphia
Difficulty with handwriting.

Dyslexia
A language-based disorder characterized by difficulties in single word decoding.

Learning Disability (LD)
A general term referring to a group of disorders that produce difficulties in listening, speaking, reading, writing, math, or spelling. These difficulties are intrinsic (internal) to the individual, and can be caused by central nervous system problems.

Learning Disorder
Any learning difficulty caused by central nervous system (brain) problems.

Neurodevelopmental Testing
Tests that assess the central nervous system to see how the child receives and processes information.

Psychoeducational Testing
Tests for brain function and academic skills.

PL94-142
Education for All Handicapped Children Act of 1975.

PL101-476
Individuals with Disabilities Educational Act of 1990 - IDEA.

PL105-17
Update of IDEA in 1997.

ADDITIONAL INFORMATION

If you have additional questions, your first source of information should be your doctor or health care provider. Additional information and other assistance can be obtained from the following organizations.

Learning Disabilities:

- **Learning Disabilities Association of America**
  4156 Library Road, Pittsburgh, PA 15234
  888-300-6710; Fax: 412-344-0224; www.ldanatl.org

- **National Center for Learning Disabilities**
  381 Park Ave. South, Suite 1401, New York, NY 10016
  888-575-7373; Fax: 212-545-9665; www.ncld.org

Attention Deficit Disorders:

- **Children with Attention Deficit Disorders (CHADD)**
  8181 Professional Place, #201, Landover, MD 20785
  800-233-4050; Fax: 301-306-7090; www.chadd.org

- **National Attention Deficit Disorder Association**
  1788 Second Street, Suite 200, Highland Park, IL 60035
  847-432-2332; www.add.org

BOOKS AND ARTICLES

Hammill, DD. A Brief Look at the Learning Disabilities Movements in the United States. *Journal of Learning Disabilities*; 25.5. May 1993: 295-310

Levine, MD, Carey, WB, Crocker, AC. *Developmental Behavioral Pediatrics. 3rd ed.* WB Saunders Company, Philadelphia, PA, 1999.

Levine, MD. *All Kinds of Minds.* Educators Publishing Service, Inc. Cambridge, MA, 1993.

Levine, MD. *Keeping a Head in School.* Educators Publishing Service, Inc. Cambridge, MA, 1990.

Lyon, GR. *Frames of Reference for the Assessment of Learning Disabilities.* Paul H. Brookes Company, Baltimore, MD, 1994.

Rief, SF. *How to Read and Teach ADD/ADHD Children.* Center for Applied Research in Education. W. Nyack, New York, NY, 1993.

NOTES